THE BASICS OF FINANCIAL MANAGEMENT

A Comprehensive Guide to Unveil the Secrets to Financial Success

HENRY ABRAHAMS

Copyright © 2024 by Henry Abrahams

All rights reserved. No part of this book may be reproduced, distributed, or transmitted in any form or by any means, including photocopying, recording, or other electronic or mechanical methods, without the prior written permission of the publisher, except in the case of brief quotations embodied in critical reviews and certain other noncommercial uses permitted by copyright law.

Unauthorized reproduction or distribution of this work is illegal and may result in civil and criminal penalties. The publisher does not assume any responsibility for third-party websites or their content that may be linked to from within this book.

Table of Contents

Foreward

Chapter 1: Introduction to financial management

Chapter 2: Basic Ideas of Finance

Chapter 3: Evaluating Choices

-Time, Risk, and Value

Chapter 4: Financial Planes

-Budgets

Chapter 5: Taxes and Tax Planning

Chapter 6: Consumer Strategies

Chapter 7: Personal Risk Management: Insurance

-Insuring Your Property

-Insuring Your Health

-Insuring Your Income

Chapter 8: Personal Risk Management: Retirement and

Estate Planning

Chapter 9: Investment Planning

Chapter 10: Behavioral Finance and Market Behavior

Chapter 11: The Practice of Investment

-Investment Information

-Investing and Trading

-Ethics and Regulation

Chapter 12: Owning Stocks

- Stocks and Stock Markets

- Stock Value

- Common Measures of Value

- Equity Strategies

Chapter 13: Investing in Mutual Funds, Commodities, Real Estate, and Collectibles

- Mutual Funds

- Real Estate Investments

- Commodities and Collectibles

Chapter 14: Career Planning

-Choosing a Job

-Finding a Job

Foreward:

In a world where financial literacy is paramount, "The Basics of Financial Management" emerges as a guiding light, illuminating the often daunting terrain of personal finance with clarity, insight, and actionable wisdom. In this era of economic uncertainty and rapid technological advancement, mastering the fundamentals of financial management is not just advantageous; it's essential for navigating life's myriad challenges and opportunities.

Within the pages of this indispensable

tome, you will embark on a journey of transformation toward financial empowerment. This book transcends mere instruction; it serves as a trusted companion, offering sage advice and practical strategies for building a solid financial foundation, regardless of one's starting point.

From budgeting and saving to investing and retirement planning, this piece covers it all with meticulous detail and unwavering clarity. No stone is left unturned as you are guided through the intricacies of managing income, expenses, debt, and assets, equipping you with the tools and knowledge needed to make informed decisions and achieve long-term financial success.

But this book is more than just a manual for managing money; it's a manifesto for reclaiming control over one's financial destiny. Through empowering anecdotes, real-life case studies, and thought-provoking exercises, you will be inspired to challenge your preconceptions, overcome your fears, and embrace a mindset of abundance and possibility.

In an age where instant gratification often takes precedence over prudent financial stewardship, this masterpiece serves as a rallying cry for a new generation of savvy consumers. It champions the virtues of patience, discipline, and foresight, reminding us that true wealth is not measured solely in dollars and cents but in peace of mind, freedom of choice, and the ability to live life on one's own terms.

As you embark on this enriching odyssey through the world of personal finance, let "The Basics of Financial Management" be your trusted compass, guiding you toward a future of prosperity, security, and fulfillment. May its wisdom serve as a beacon of hope and empowerment, illuminating the path to financial mastery and unlocking the boundless potential that lies within each and every one of us.

Chapter 1:

Introduction to financial management

In the dynamic world of business, financial management stands as a cornerstone for organizational success. This introductory chapter sets the stage by elucidating the fundamental concepts and principles that underpin financial management.

1. **Understanding Financial**

Management: Financial management encompasses the art and science of efficiently managing a company's financial resources to achieve its objectives. It involves planning, organizing, directing, and controlling the financial activities of an organization.

2. Objectives of Financial Management: The primary goal of financial management is to maximize shareholder wealth by ensuring the optimal utilization of funds. This entails making strategic decisions to enhance profitability, liquidity, and solvency while minimizing risks.

3. Scope of Financial Management: Financial management covers a broad spectrum of activities, including financial planning, budgeting, investment decisions, financing decisions, and risk management. It also entails the analysis of financial statements and performance metrics to evaluate the financial health of an organization.

4. Key Financial Concepts: This section introduces essential financial concepts such as time value of money, risk and return, cost of capital, and financial markets. Understanding these concepts is crucial for making informed financial decisions and assessing the impact of various financial strategies.

5. Role of Financial Managers: Financial managers play a pivotal role in steering the financial affairs of an organization. They are responsible for formulating financial policies, managing cash flows, raising capital, and assessing investment opportunities. Their expertise is instrumental in achieving the financial objectives of the organization.

6. Ethical and Legal Considerations: Financial management operates within a framework of ethical and legal principles. Practitioners are required to adhere to ethical standards and comply with regulatory requirements to maintain transparency, integrity, and accountability in financial operations.

7. Challenges and Opportunities: The chapter concludes by highlighting the challenges and opportunities facing financial managers in today's dynamic business environment. From technological advancements to global economic fluctuations, financial management demands adaptability and innovation to navigate through uncertainties and capitalize on emerging trends.

By providing a comprehensive overview of financial management, this chapter lays the foundation for a deeper exploration into the intricacies of managing financial resources effectively to drive organizational and personal success.

Chapter 2:

Basic Ideas of Finance

Finance, as a discipline, encompasses a multitude of concepts, theories, and principles that form the foundation of modern financial management. In this chapter, we delve into the basic ideas of finance, elucidating key concepts that underpin financial decision-making and resource allocation within organizations.

1. Time Value of Money: At the heart

of financial theory lies the principle of the time value of money. This fundamental concept posits that a dollar today is worth more than a dollar in the future due to the opportunity cost of delayed consumption and the potential to earn returns through investment. Understanding the time value of money enables financial managers to assess the present and future value of cash flows, make informed investment decisions, and evaluate the profitability of projects.

2. Risk and Return: Finance operates within the realm of uncertainty, where investment decisions entail a trade-off between risk and return. Higher returns are typically associated with higher levels of risk, as investors demand compensation for bearing uncertainty. Financial managers employ various risk management techniques, such as diversification, hedging, and insurance, to mitigate risk and optimize the risk-return profile of investment portfolios.

3. Cost of Capital: The cost of capital represents the minimum rate of return required by investors to compensate for the risk of investing in a particular asset or project. It encompasses both the cost of equity and the cost of debt, reflecting the opportunity cost of funds employed in financing activities. Financial managers utilize the cost of capital as a benchmark for evaluating investment opportunities, determining the optimal capital structure, and assessing the financial viability of projects.

4. Financial Markets and Institutions: Financial markets serve as the conduits through which funds are channeled from savers to investors, facilitating the efficient allocation of capital in the economy. These markets encompass a diverse array of instruments, including stocks, bonds, derivatives, and commodities, each catering to distinct investor preferences and risk profiles. Financial institutions, such as banks, investment firms, and insurance companies, play a vital role in intermediating between surplus and deficit units, providing liquidity, and facilitating the transfer of financial assets.

5. Financial Statements Analysis: Financial statements serve as the primary source of information for assessing the financial performance and position of an organization. Key financial statements include the balance sheet, income statement, and cash flow statement, each providing insights into different aspects of the firm's operations, profitability, and liquidity. Financial managers employ various analytical tools and ratios, such as profitability ratios, liquidity ratios, and leverage ratios, to interpret financial statements, identify trends, and gauge the financial health of the organization.

6. Capital Budgeting: Capital budgeting entails the process of evaluating and selecting long-term investment projects that yield positive returns and create value for the organization. Financial managers utilize techniques such as net present value (NPV), internal rate of return (IRR), and payback period to assess the profitability, risk, and feasibility of investment opportunities. Effective capital budgeting facilitates strategic decision-making, optimal resource allocation, and long-term growth for the organization.

7. Financial Planning and Forecasting: Financial planning involves the formulation of comprehensive financial plans and budgets that align with the strategic objectives of the organization. It encompasses forecasting future cash flows, revenues, and expenses, as well as identifying funding requirements and capital expenditure priorities. Financial managers employ forecasting techniques, such as trend analysis, regression analysis, and scenario analysis, to anticipate future financial performance and devise proactive strategies to achieve organizational goals.

8. Corporate Governance and Ethics: Corporate governance encompasses the mechanisms, processes, and structures that govern the behavior of corporate entities and ensure accountability, transparency, and fairness in decision-making. Ethical considerations are integral to financial management practices, guiding ethical behavior, integrity, and social responsibility in the conduct of financial transactions and operations. Financial managers are entrusted with upholding ethical standards, complying with regulatory requirements, and safeguarding the interests of stakeholders.

By elucidating these fundamental ideas of finance, this chapter lays the groundwork for a deeper understanding of financial management principles and practices. Armed with this knowledge, readers are equipped to navigate the complexities of financial decision-making, allocate resources effectively, and foster sustainable growth and prosperity within their organizations.

Chapter 3:

Evaluating Choices

- Time, Risk, and Value

In the realm of financial management, understanding the interplay between time, risk, and value is paramount. These three concepts form the bedrock upon which sound financial decisions are made, influencing everything from investment strategies to capital budgeting. This comprehensive exploration delves into the intricate dynamics of time, risk, and value, shedding light on their significance and implications in the field of finance.

Time:

Time is a fundamental dimension in financial management, serving as a critical factor in various aspects of decision-making. The concept of time value of money (TVM) lies at the heart of financial analysis, recognizing that a dollar received today holds more value than a dollar received in the future due to the potential for investment and earning returns. This principle underpins techniques such as discounted cash flow analysis, net present value (NPV), and internal rate of return (IRR), enabling businesses to evaluate the profitability and feasibility of projects over time.

Furthermore, time horizons play a crucial role in investment planning and risk management. Investors must consider their investment goals, timeframes, and risk tolerance when constructing portfolios to optimize returns while mitigating potential losses. Short-term investments may offer liquidity and flexibility but often entail higher volatility, while long-term investments can capitalize on compounding returns but require patience and a tolerance for market fluctuations. Understanding the time dimension allows financial managers to align investment strategies with organizational objectives and stakeholders' preferences effectively.

Risk:

Risk permeates every financial decision, encompassing uncertainties and potential adverse outcomes that could impact the achievement of objectives. From market volatility to credit default, operational failures to regulatory changes, businesses face a myriad of risks that must be identified, assessed, and managed effectively. Risk management frameworks provide methodologies for quantifying risk exposure, evaluating risk-return trade-offs, and implementing strategies to mitigate or transfer risks.

Different types of risk, including market risk, credit risk, liquidity risk, operational risk, and systemic risk, demand tailored approaches to risk management. Diversification, hedging, insurance, and derivative instruments are among the tools utilized to hedge against specific risks and safeguard financial stability. Moreover, risk-adjusted return metrics such as the Sharpe ratio and the Sortino ratio enable investors to evaluate the efficiency of portfolios in generating returns relative to the level of risk undertaken.

Value:

Value creation lies at the core of financial management, encapsulating the ability to generate returns in excess of the cost of capital and enhance shareholders' wealth. While financial value is quantifiable through metrics such as earnings per share (EPS), return on investment (ROI), and economic value added (EVA), it encompasses broader dimensions beyond monetary gains. Non-financial value drivers, including brand reputation, customer satisfaction, employee engagement, and corporate social responsibility, contribute to long-term sustainability and competitive advantage.

Strategic decisions regarding investment, financing, and dividend policies are guided by the pursuit of value maximization, balancing short-term profitability with long-term growth objectives. Financial managers must assess investment opportunities based on their potential to create value, considering factors such as cash flows, risk-adjusted returns, and strategic fit within the organization's portfolio. Effective capital allocation ensures that resources are allocated to projects with the highest potential for value creation, optimizing the overall performance and resilience of the business.

To wrap up, time, risk, and value are intricately intertwined concepts that shape the landscape of financial management, influencing decision-making processes and outcomes. By recognizing the significance of these dimensions and employing robust analytical frameworks, financial managers can navigate uncertainties, capitalize on opportunities, and enhance shareholder wealth in an evolving economic environment. A holistic understanding of time, risk, and value is indispensable for fostering sustainable growth, resilience, and competitiveness in today's dynamic marketplace.

Chapter 4: Financial Plans

-Budgets

This chapter delves into the indispensable components of financial plans, with a particular focus on budgets. Financial plans serve as roadmaps for organizations, outlining strategies, objectives, and resource allocations to achieve financial stability and growth. Within this chapter, we explore the intricacies of budgeting, a cornerstone of effective financial management, and its role in guiding decision-making, resource allocation, and performance evaluation.

Understanding Financial Plans:

Financial plans encompass a comprehensive set of documents that articulate an organization's financial goals, strategies, and tactics. These plans typically include components such as income statements, balance sheets, cash flow projections, and capital expenditure plans, providing stakeholders with insights into the organization's financial health and future prospects. By aligning financial plans with strategic objectives, organizations can enhance transparency, accountability, and operational efficiency, fostering informed decision-making and stakeholder confidence.

The Importance of Budgets:

Budgets represent detailed financial plans that allocate resources to specific activities, departments, or projects within an organization. They serve as quantitative expressions of strategic priorities, setting targets for revenue generation, expense management, and investment allocation. Budgets facilitate resource optimization by establishing spending limits, identifying cost-saving opportunities, and aligning expenditures with revenue expectations. Moreover, budgets enable performance monitoring and variance analysis, empowering managers to identify deviations from planned outcomes and take corrective actions as needed.

Types of Budgets:

Various types of budgets are utilized across different organizations, each tailored to suit specific operational contexts and strategic objectives. Common types of budgets include:

1. Operating Budgets: These budgets outline the expected revenues and expenses associated with day-to-day operations, including sales forecasts, production costs, and administrative expenses. Operating budgets serve as the foundation for short-term financial planning and control, enabling managers to monitor performance against predetermined targets and adjust operations accordingly.

2. Capital Budgets: Capital budgets focus on long-term investment decisions, including expenditures on assets such as equipment, machinery, and infrastructure. These budgets

evaluate the feasibility and profitability of capital projects, considering factors such as upfront costs, expected cash flows, and the cost of capital. Capital budgets play a crucial role in strategic planning, guiding investment prioritization and resource allocation to support organizational growth and competitiveness.

3. Cash Budgets: Cash budgets forecast the organization's cash inflows and outflows over a specific period, providing insights into liquidity management and cash flow dynamics. By projecting cash requirements and identifying potential cash shortages or

surpluses, cash budgets enable managers to optimize cash utilization, manage working capital effectively, and mitigate liquidity risks.

4. Flexible Budgets: Flexible budgets adjust for changes in activity levels or business conditions, allowing for dynamic resource allocation and performance evaluation. Unlike static budgets, which are fixed regardless of fluctuations in output or sales volumes, flexible budgets adapt to variations in production levels, sales revenues, or other performance metrics. This flexibility enhances managerial decision-making by providing a more

accurate representation of costs and revenues at different levels of activity.

Budgeting Process:

The budgeting process encompasses several key steps, from setting financial objectives to monitoring and evaluating performance. These steps typically include:

1. Goal Setting: Establishing clear and measurable financial objectives that align with the organization's strategic priorities and operational needs.

2. Data Collection and Analysis: Gathering relevant financial and operational data to inform budget

assumptions, forecasts, and resource requirements.

3. Budget Formulation: Developing detailed budgets for revenue, expenses, and investments based on the organization's goals, priorities, and available resources.

4. Review and Approval: Reviewing budget proposals, soliciting feedback from stakeholders, and obtaining approval from senior management or governing bodies.

5. Implementation: Communicating budget targets to relevant departments or units, allocating

resources accordingly, and initiating budget execution activities.

6. Monitoring and Control: Tracking actual performance against budgeted targets, analyzing variances, and taking corrective actions to address deviations and improve financial outcomes.

7. Performance Evaluation: Assessing the effectiveness of budgeting processes, identifying lessons learned, and making adjustments to enhance future planning and control efforts.

In the end Chapter 4 of "The Basics of Financial Management" underscores the critical role of financial plans and budgets in guiding organizations toward fiscal success. By developing comprehensive financial plans and leveraging effective budgeting techniques, organizations can enhance financial transparency, accountability, and performance, positioning themselves for sustainable growth and resilience in today's dynamic business environment. With careful planning, diligent execution, and continuous monitoring, financial managers can navigate the complexities of budgeting and achieve their strategic objectives with confidence and precision.

Chapter 5:

Taxes and Tax Planning

This chapter delves into the intricate world of taxes and tax planning, essential components of financial decision-making for individuals and organizations alike. Taxes represent a significant financial burden and regulatory obligation, impacting income, investments, and business operations. Within this chapter, we explore the multifaceted aspects of taxation, strategies for tax planning, and the implications for financial management and wealth accumulation.

Understanding Taxes:

Taxes are compulsory levies imposed by governments on individuals, businesses, and other entities to finance public expenditures and services. The tax landscape encompasses various types of taxes, including income taxes, corporate taxes, sales taxes, property taxes, and excise taxes, each with its own rules, rates, and compliance requirements. Understanding the nuances of taxation is essential for individuals and organizations to optimize their tax liabilities, minimize risks, and comply with legal obligations.

Key Concepts in Taxation:

Several key concepts underpin the taxation framework, shaping the calculation, assessment, and payment of taxes. These concepts include:

1. Taxable Income: Taxable income refers to the portion of an individual's or entity's income that is subject to taxation after accounting for allowable deductions, exemptions, and credits. Understanding what constitutes

taxable income is crucial for determining tax liabilities and optimizing tax planning strategies.

2. Tax Rates: Tax rates represent the percentage of taxable income that individuals or entities must pay in taxes. Tax rates vary depending on the type of income (e.g., ordinary income, capital gains), filing status (e.g., single, married filing jointly), and tax jurisdiction (e.g., federal, state, local). Knowledge of applicable tax rates enables taxpayers to estimate their tax liabilities accurately and plan accordingly.

3. Tax Deductions and Credits: Tax

deductions and credits provide opportunities for taxpayers to reduce their taxable income or offset tax liabilities. Deductions, such as those for mortgage interest, charitable contributions, and business expenses, reduce taxable income before calculating taxes owed. Tax credits, on the other hand, directly reduce the amount of tax owed, dollar for dollar. Leveraging deductions and credits effectively can significantly lower tax burdens and improve financial outcomes.

Tax Planning Strategies:

Tax planning involves the proactive

management of financial affairs to minimize tax liabilities, maximize tax benefits, and achieve long-term financial goals. Effective tax planning strategies encompass a range of approaches, including:

1. Income Shifting: Income shifting involves redistributing income among family members or entities to take advantage of lower tax brackets, deductions, or exemptions. Strategies such as gifting, income splitting, and asset transfers can help optimize tax outcomes and preserve wealth across generations.

2. Retirement Planning: Retirement

planning incorporates tax-efficient strategies for accumulating savings, managing retirement accounts, and withdrawing funds during retirement. Contributions to tax-advantaged retirement plans, such as 401(k)s and IRAs, offer immediate tax benefits, while Roth accounts provide tax-free withdrawals in retirement. Additionally, strategic timing of retirement distributions and Social Security benefits can minimize tax liabilities and maximize retirement income.

3. Investment Planning: Investment planning involves selecting tax-efficient investment vehicles, asset

allocation strategies, and capital gains management techniques to optimize after-tax returns. Tax-advantaged investments, such as municipal bonds and retirement accounts, offer preferential tax treatment, while tax-loss harvesting and tax-deferred exchanges can mitigate capital gains taxes and enhance investment performance.

4. Estate Planning: Estate planning encompasses strategies for preserving and transferring wealth to future generations while minimizing estate taxes and probate costs. Techniques such as lifetime gifts,

trusts, and charitable bequests can reduce estate tax liabilities and ensure efficient wealth transfer according to the individual's wishes.

By understanding the principles of taxation, leveraging tax planning strategies, and complying with legal obligations, individuals and organizations can optimize their tax outcomes, minimize risks, and achieve their financial objectives with confidence and efficiency. With careful consideration of tax implications and proactive planning, taxpayers can navigate the complexities of the tax system and enhance their financial well-being in the pursuit of long-term prosperity and security.

Chapter 6:

Consumer Strategies

This chapter explores consumer strategies, focusing on the fundamental principles and best practices that individuals can employ to make informed financial decisions. From budgeting and saving to borrowing and investing, consumers face a myriad of choices that impact their financial well-being and future prospects. This chapter delves into the strategies and tools available to consumers to optimize their financial outcomes and achieve their goals.

Understanding Consumer Behavior:

Consumer behavior encompasses the actions, preferences, and decision-making processes that individuals exhibit when acquiring, using, and disposing of goods and services. Understanding consumer behavior is essential for financial managers, marketers, and policymakers to anticipate trends, tailor products and services, and promote financial literacy and empowerment. Key factors influencing consumer behavior include psychological, social, cultural, and economic variables, which shape attitudes toward money, risk tolerance, spending habits, and savings behavior.

Budgeting and Saving:

Budgeting is the foundation of sound financial management, enabling individuals to allocate income effectively, prioritize expenses, and achieve financial goals. A budget serves as a roadmap for managing cash flow, tracking expenditures, and building savings over time. By creating a budget that aligns income with expenses and incorporates savings goals, consumers can establish healthy financial habits, avoid overspending, and accumulate wealth for emergencies, retirement, and other long-term objectives.

Saving strategies encompass various approaches to building financial reserves and achieving short-term and long-term financial goals. These strategies include:

1. Automatic Savings: Setting up automatic transfers from checking to savings accounts or utilizing payroll deductions to automate savings contributions.

2. Emergency Fund: Establishing an

emergency fund to cover unexpected expenses, such as medical bills, car repairs, or job loss. Financial experts recommend saving three to six months' worth of living expenses in an easily accessible account.

3. Goal-Based Saving: Setting specific savings goals, such as purchasing a home, funding education, or traveling, and allocating resources accordingly. Breaking down larger goals into manageable milestones can help individuals stay motivated and track progress over time.

4. Retirement Saving: Contributing to employer-sponsored retirement plans,

such as 401(k)s or individual retirement accounts (IRAs), to build retirement savings and take advantage of tax benefits and employer matches. Consistent contributions and diversified investments are key to achieving long-term retirement goals.

Borrowing and Debt Management:

Borrowing is a common financial tool that individuals use to finance purchases, investments, education, and other expenses. However, prudent borrowing and effective debt management are essential to avoid excessive debt burdens and financial strain. Strategies for responsible borrowing and debt management include:

1. Debt Evaluation: Assessing current debt obligations, including outstanding balances, interest rates, and repayment terms, to understand the total debt burden and prioritize repayment strategies.

2. Debt Repayment Plans: Developing a repayment plan to pay off debts systematically, focusing on high-interest debt first or utilizing debt snowball or debt avalanche methods to accelerate debt payoff.

3. Credit Management: Monitoring

credit reports regularly, managing credit card usage responsibly, and avoiding late payments or excessive credit inquiries to maintain a positive credit score and access favorable borrowing terms.

4. Debt Consolidation: Consolidating multiple debts into a single loan with a lower interest rate or more favorable terms to simplify repayment and reduce overall interest costs.

Investing and Wealth Building:

Investing plays a critical role in wealth accumulation and financial security, enabling individuals to grow their assets over time and achieve long-term financial goals. Consumer investment strategies encompass various approaches to portfolio construction, asset allocation, and risk management, including:

1. Goal-Based Investing: Aligning investment strategies with specific financial goals, time horizons, and risk tolerance levels. Different goals may require different investment approaches, such as growth-oriented strategies for long-term objectives and income-focused strategies for retirement income.

2. Diversification: Spreading

investments across different asset classes, sectors, and geographic regions to reduce portfolio risk and enhance risk-adjusted returns. Diversification can help mitigate the impact of market volatility and unexpected events on investment performance.

3. Tax-Efficient Investing: Implementing tax-efficient investment strategies, such as utilizing tax-advantaged retirement accounts, harvesting tax losses, and optimizing asset location, to minimize tax liabilities and maximize after-tax returns.

4. Long-Term Perspective: Maintaining a long-term investment perspective and avoiding reactionary or emotional responses to short-term market fluctuations. Consistent contributions, disciplined rebalancing, and staying focused on long-term financial goals are key to successful investing.

By adopting prudent budgeting and saving habits, managing debt responsibly, and implementing sound investment strategies, consumers can navigate financial challenges, capitalize on opportunities, and build wealth over time. Empowered with knowledge and equipped with effective financial tools and resources, individuals can take control of their financial futures and pursue their goals with confidence and resilience.

Chapter 7:

Personal Risk Management: Insurance

-Insuring Your Property

I will give comprehensive insights into the importance of property insurance, strategies for selecting appropriate coverage, and measures to mitigate risks associated with property ownership. Whether safeguarding a home, business premises, or valuable assets, property insurance plays a crucial role in protecting against financial losses due to unforeseen events such as natural disasters, accidents, theft, or liability claims. This chapter explores the various facets of property insurance, empowering readers to make informed decisions to safeguard their assets and financial well-being.

Understanding Property Insurance:

Property insurance is a contractual arrangement between an insurer and a policyholder, wherein the insurer agrees to compensate the policyholder for covered losses or damages to the insured property in exchange for premium payments. Property insurance policies provide financial protection against a wide range of perils, including fire, theft, vandalism, windstorm, hail, and water damage, depending on the specific terms and conditions of the policy. By transferring the risk of property loss to an insurance provider, policyholders can mitigate financial exposure and ensure financial stability in the event of property damage or destruction.

Types of Property Insurance:

Property insurance encompasses various types of coverage tailored to meet the diverse needs of individuals, homeowners, renters, landlords, and businesses. Some common types of property insurance include:

1. Homeowners Insurance: Homeowners insurance provides coverage for residential properties, including single-family homes, condominiums, and townhouses. Policies typically include coverage for the dwelling structure, personal belongings, liability protection, and additional living expenses in case of temporary displacement due to covered perils.

2. Renters Insurance: Renters

insurance offers protection for tenants renting residential properties, covering personal belongings, liability claims, and additional living expenses similar to homeowners insurance. Renters insurance is essential for renters to protect their belongings and liability risks, as the landlord's insurance typically does not cover tenant possessions.

3. Commercial Property Insurance: Commercial property insurance safeguards business properties, including buildings, equipment, inventory, and fixtures, against damage or loss due to covered perils.

Commercial property policies may also include business interruption coverage, which compensates for lost income and operating expenses during periods of property damage or disruption.

4. Landlord Insurance: Landlord insurance provides coverage for property owners renting out residential or commercial properties to tenants. In addition to property damage coverage, landlord insurance may include liability protection, rental income reimbursement, and coverage for legal expenses related to tenant disputes or property damage claims.

5. Specialty Property Insurance: Specialty property insurance policies offer coverage for unique or high-value properties, such as vacation homes, luxury estates, historic buildings, fine art collections, jewelry, and valuable possessions. These policies are tailored to address specific risks and may include higher coverage limits and specialized endorsements for unique assets.

Factors Influencing Property Insurance Premiums:

Several factors influence property insurance premiums, including:

1. Property Characteristics: The type, age, location, size, construction materials, and features of the insured property, such as security systems, fire sprinklers, and protective devices, impact insurance premiums. Properties located in high-risk areas prone to natural disasters or crime may attract higher premiums.

2. Coverage Limits and Deductibles: The amount of coverage selected and the deductible chosen by the policyholder affect insurance premiums. Higher coverage limits and lower deductibles typically result in higher premiums, while lower

coverage limits and higher deductibles may reduce premiums but increase out-of-pocket expenses in the event of a claim.

3. Insurance History: The policyholder's claims history, credit score, insurance coverage history, and prior losses may influence insurance premiums. A history of frequent claims or poor credit may lead to higher premiums, while a clean claims history and strong credit may qualify for lower rates.

4. Risk Mitigation Measures: Implementing risk mitigation measures, such as installing security

systems, smoke detectors, fire alarms, and storm shutters, may qualify for insurance discounts or premium reductions. Insurance providers often offer incentives for proactive risk management and loss prevention efforts.

Strategies for Property Insurance Planning:

Effective property insurance planning involves assessing insurance needs, comparing coverage options, and implementing risk management strategies to optimize coverage and minimize costs. Key strategies for property insurance planning include:

1. Assessing Insurance Needs: Conducting a thorough assessment of property risks, asset values, and coverage requirements is essential to determine the appropriate type and level of insurance coverage. Evaluating potential perils, liability exposures, and financial vulnerabilities helps identify gaps in coverage and mitigate risks effectively.

2. Reviewing Policy Coverage: Reviewing insurance policy terms, conditions, exclusions, and coverage limits is crucial to ensure adequate protection and avoid surprises in the event of a claim. Policyholders should

understand what is covered, what is excluded, and any limitations or endorsements that may affect coverage.

3. Comparing Insurance Quotes: Shopping around and comparing insurance quotes from multiple providers allows policyholders to find competitive rates, favorable terms, and quality coverage options. Working with an independent insurance agent or broker can help navigate the complexities of insurance policies and obtain personalized recommendations tailored to individual needs.

4. Bundling Policies: Bundling multiple

insurance policies, such as homeowners, auto, and umbrella insurance, with the same insurer often results in discounts or multi-policy savings. Consolidating insurance coverage under a single provider can simplify billing, streamline claims processing, and save money on premiums.

5. Reviewing Coverage Periodically: Regularly reviewing insurance coverage and reassessing insurance needs is essential to adapt to changing circumstances, property values, and risk exposures. Life events such as home renovations, property

acquisitions, or changes in family status may necessitate adjustments to insurance coverage to ensure adequate protection.

Conclusion:

In conclusion, insuring property is a critical component of financial planning and risk management, providing essential protection against unforeseen events and financial losses. By understanding the types of property insurance available, factors influencing insurance premiums, and strategies for insurance planning, individuals, homeowners, renters, landlords, and businesses can make informed decisions to safeguard their assets and financial well-being. With comprehensive insurance coverage and proactive risk management, property owners can gain peace of mind knowing that their investments are protected and their financial futures are secure against unexpected perils.

-Insuring Your Health

Health insurance plays a pivotal role in safeguarding individuals and families against the financial burden of medical expenses, ensuring access to essential healthcare services and promoting overall well-being. This chapter provides readers with a comprehensive understanding of health insurance options, considerations for plan selection, and proactive measures to manage healthcare costs effectively.

Understanding Health Insurance:

Health insurance is a contractual arrangement between an insurer and a policyholder, providing financial protection against the costs of medical care and treatment. Health insurance policies vary in coverage scope, benefits, cost-sharing arrangements, and provider networks, offering individuals and families access to essential healthcare services, including doctor visits, hospitalization, prescription drugs, preventive care, and emergency treatment. By pooling risk and spreading financial liability across a large population, health insurance helps mitigate the financial impact of unexpected medical expenses and promotes access to timely and appropriate healthcare.

Types of Health Insurance Coverage:

Health insurance coverage encompasses various types of plans and programs designed to meet the diverse needs of individuals, families, and employers. Common types of health insurance coverage include:

1. Employer-Sponsored Health Insurance: Employer-sponsored health insurance plans are offered by employers to their employees as part of employee benefits packages. These plans may include options such as health maintenance organizations (HMOs), preferred provider organizations (PPOs), point of service (POS) plans, or high-deductible health plans (HDHPs) with health savings accounts (HSAs). Employer-sponsored health insurance often provides group coverage at

discounted rates, with employers subsidizing a portion of the premiums.

2. Individual and Family Health Insurance: Individual and family health insurance plans are purchased directly by individuals or families from insurance companies or through health insurance marketplaces. These plans offer coverage for individuals and their dependents and may include options such as comprehensive coverage, catastrophic coverage, or short-term coverage. Individuals and families can choose from a range of plan options based on their healthcare needs, budget, and preferences.

3. Government-Sponsored Health Insurance: Government-sponsored health insurance programs provide coverage for eligible individuals and populations, including Medicare for seniors and people with disabilities, Medicaid for low-income individuals and families, and the Children's Health Insurance Program (CHIP) for children from low-income families. These programs aim to expand access to healthcare services and provide financial assistance to vulnerable populations who may not have access to employer-sponsored or individual health insurance coverage.

4. Health Savings Accounts (HSAs) and Flexible Spending Accounts (FSAs): Health savings accounts (HSAs) and flexible spending accounts (FSAs) are tax-advantaged savings vehicles that allow individuals to set aside pre-tax funds to pay for qualified medical expenses. HSAs are available to individuals with high-deductible health plans (HDHPs) and offer triple tax benefits (tax-deductible contributions, tax-free growth, and tax-free withdrawals for qualified medical expenses). FSAs are offered by employers and allow employees to contribute pre-tax dollars to cover eligible medical expenses not covered

by insurance.

Considerations for Health Insurance Planning:

Effective health insurance planning involves assessing healthcare needs, comparing plan options, and selecting coverage that aligns with individual and family priorities. Key considerations for health insurance planning include:

1. Coverage Needs: Assessing healthcare needs, including anticipated medical expenses, prescription drug requirements, chronic conditions, and preventive

care services, is essential to determine the appropriate level of coverage. Individuals and families should consider factors such as age, health status, lifestyle, and family size when evaluating coverage needs.

2. Network Access: Evaluating provider networks, including primary care physicians, specialists, hospitals, and pharmacies, is crucial to ensure access to preferred healthcare providers and facilities. In-network providers typically offer lower out-of-pocket costs, while out-of-network providers may result in higher costs or limited coverage.

3. Cost Sharing: Understanding cost-sharing arrangements, including premiums, deductibles, copayments, and coinsurance, helps individuals and families estimate out-of-pocket expenses and budget accordingly. Balancing monthly premiums with out-of-pocket costs is essential to find a plan that offers affordable coverage without sacrificing access to necessary healthcare services.

4. Plan Features and Benefits: Reviewing plan features, benefits, coverage exclusions, and limitations is essential to understand the scope of coverage and potential restrictions.

Individuals and families should assess coverage for preventive care, prescription drugs, specialist visits, hospitalization, emergency care, and other essential services to ensure comprehensive protection.

5. Financial Assistance Options: Exploring financial assistance options, such as premium subsidies, cost-sharing reductions, or public health insurance programs, may help individuals and families access affordable coverage and reduce out-of-pocket expenses. Eligibility criteria for financial assistance programs vary based on income, household size, and

other factors, so it's important to explore available options and apply for assistance if eligible.

Health insurance is a critical component of financial planning and risk management, providing essential protection against the costs of medical care and treatment. By understanding the types of health insurance coverage available, evaluating coverage needs, and comparing plan options, individuals and families can make informed decisions to safeguard their health and financial well-being. With comprehensive health insurance coverage and proactive healthcare management, individuals and families can access necessary healthcare services, manage healthcare costs effectively, and achieve greater peace of mind knowing that their health and financial futures are protected against unexpected medical expenses.

-Insuring Your Income

Income is a vital asset that supports individuals and families' financial obligations, including daily expenses, debt repayments, savings contributions, and long-term financial goals. This part provides you with a comprehensive understanding of income insurance options, considerations for policy selection, and proactive measures to mitigate income risk effectively.

Understanding Income Protection:

Income protection insurance is designed to provide financial support to individuals and families in the event of income loss due to illness, injury, disability, or unemployment. Income protection policies offer a source of replacement income to cover living expenses, maintain financial stability, and sustain quality of life during periods of incapacity or job loss. By transferring the risk of income loss to an insurance provider, policyholders can mitigate financial vulnerability and ensure continuity of financial support in challenging circumstances.

Types of Income Protection Insurance:

Income protection insurance encompasses various types of policies and coverage options tailored to meet the diverse needs of individuals, professionals, and workers in different occupations. Common types of income protection insurance include:

1. Disability Insurance: Disability insurance provides income

replacement benefits to individuals who are unable to work due to illness, injury, or disability. Disability insurance policies may offer short-term or long-term coverage, with benefits typically based on a percentage of the insured individual's pre-disability earnings. Disability insurance can be obtained through employer-sponsored group plans, individual policies, or government disability programs.

2. Unemployment Insurance: Unemployment insurance offers temporary financial assistance to individuals who lose their jobs through no fault of their own and meet

eligibility criteria for unemployment benefits. Unemployment insurance benefits are administered by state governments and provide partial income replacement for a limited duration, typically up to 26 weeks, to help unemployed workers cover living expenses while seeking new employment opportunities.

3. Critical Illness Insurance: Critical illness insurance pays a lump-sum benefit to policyholders diagnosed with covered critical illnesses or medical conditions, such as cancer, heart attack, stroke, or organ failure. Critical illness insurance provides

financial support to cover medical expenses, treatment costs, and other financial obligations during recovery from a serious illness, allowing individuals to focus on their health and well-being without financial stress.

4. Income Continuation Insurance: Income continuation insurance offers supplementary income benefits to individuals during periods of temporary disability or partial incapacity, allowing them to maintain financial stability and cover living expenses while recovering from injury or illness. Income continuation insurance policies may provide

benefits in addition to disability insurance coverage or as standalone coverage for specific income protection needs.

Considerations for Income Protection Planning:

Effective income protection planning involves evaluating income risks, assessing insurance needs, and selecting coverage options that provide adequate financial support during income loss or interruption. Key considerations for income protection planning include:

1. Income Replacement Needs:

Estimating income replacement needs, including monthly living expenses, debt obligations, savings contributions, and other financial commitments, is essential to determine the appropriate level of coverage. Individuals and families should assess their current income sources, expenses, and lifestyle preferences to identify gaps in income protection and address potential financial vulnerabilities.

2. Coverage Duration: Considering the duration of coverage needed, such as short-term or long-term disability benefits, temporary unemployment benefits, or critical illness lump-sum

payments, helps individuals and families tailor coverage to their specific income protection needs. Short-term coverage may suffice for temporary income interruptions, while long-term coverage provides sustained financial support for extended periods of incapacity or job loss.

3. Benefit Amount and Waiting Period: Determining the benefit amount and waiting period for insurance coverage involves balancing affordability with adequate protection. Policyholders should select benefit amounts that align with their income replacement

needs and financial obligations, while choosing waiting periods that balance premium costs with timely access to benefits.

4. Policy Features and Riders: Reviewing policy features, exclusions, limitations, and optional riders is crucial to understanding the scope of coverage and customizing insurance protection to individual preferences. Optional riders, such as cost-of-living adjustments (COLAs), partial disability benefits, and return-of-premium riders, offer additional flexibility and enhanced coverage options to meet evolving needs.

5. Coordination with Other Benefits: Coordinating income protection insurance benefits with other sources of financial support, such as employer benefits, social security disability benefits, workers' compensation, or savings and investments, helps optimize income replacement and minimize financial gaps during periods of income loss. Understanding how insurance benefits interact with other benefits and income sources ensures comprehensive coverage and effective financial planning.

Insuring income is a critical component of financial planning and risk management, providing essential protection against the financial consequences of income loss or interruption. By understanding the types of income protection insurance available, assessing income replacement needs, and selecting coverage options that align with individual preferences and circumstances, individuals and families can safeguard their financial stability and security in the face of unforeseen events. With comprehensive income protection coverage and proactive risk management, individuals can achieve greater peace of mind knowing that their income and financial well-being are protected against unexpected challenges and disruptions.

Chapter 8:

Personal Risk Management: Retirement and Estate Planning

Now let's delve into the critical aspects of personal risk management, focusing on retirement planning and estate planning. As individuals progress through different life stages, it becomes imperative to assess and manage risks associated with financial security, retirement readiness, and estate preservation. This chapter explores the key components of retirement and estate planning, strategies for wealth accumulation and distribution, and measures to ensure long-term financial well-being.

Retirement Planning:

Retirement planning is a fundamental aspect of personal financial management, ensuring individuals have the financial resources to support their desired lifestyle during retirement years. Effective retirement planning involves setting retirement goals, estimating retirement income needs, and implementing strategies to accumulate savings and investments to achieve those goals. Key components of retirement planning include:

1. Retirement Income Needs: Estimating retirement income needs involves evaluating current expenses, lifestyle preferences, healthcare costs, inflationary trends, and expected retirement duration. By determining the desired retirement lifestyle and projecting future expenses, individuals can establish realistic income targets for retirement planning purposes.

2. Retirement Savings Vehicles:

Selecting appropriate retirement savings vehicles, such as employer-sponsored retirement plans (e.g., 401(k), 403(b)), individual retirement accounts (IRAs), Roth IRAs, and annuities, is essential to build retirement assets efficiently. Each retirement savings vehicle offers unique tax advantages, contribution limits, investment options, and withdrawal rules, allowing individuals to tailor their retirement savings strategies to their specific needs and circumstances.

3. Investment Strategies: Implementing investment strategies

that align with retirement goals, risk tolerance, and time horizon is crucial to grow retirement savings over time. Diversification, asset allocation, and risk management techniques help individuals build a well-balanced investment portfolio that maximizes returns while minimizing volatility and downside risk. Regular contributions, systematic investing, and periodic portfolio rebalancing are key to achieving long-term investment success.

4. Retirement Income Sources: Identifying and optimizing retirement income sources, including Social

Security benefits, pensions, retirement savings, investment income, and part-time employment, is essential to create a sustainable income stream during retirement. Maximizing Social Security benefits, coordinating pension distributions, and implementing withdrawal strategies from retirement accounts help individuals optimize retirement income and minimize tax liabilities.

Estate Planning:

Estate planning involves the orderly transfer of assets and wealth to intended beneficiaries while minimizing estate taxes, probate costs, and family disputes. Effective estate planning ensures that individuals' wishes are carried out regarding asset distribution, guardianship arrangements, healthcare directives, and charitable bequests. Key components of estate planning include:

1. Will and Testament: Drafting a will is a foundational element of estate planning, providing instructions for asset distribution, appointment of guardians for minor children, and nomination of executors to administer the estate. A properly executed will ensures that assets are distributed

according to the individual's wishes and minimizes the risk of intestacy, where state laws dictate asset distribution.

2. Trusts: Establishing trusts allows individuals to transfer assets to designated beneficiaries while retaining control over asset distribution, minimizing probate costs, and providing asset protection benefits. Trusts can be utilized for various estate planning objectives, such as asset preservation, minor children's education funding, charitable giving, and special needs planning.

3. Beneficiary Designations: Reviewing and updating beneficiary designations on retirement accounts, life insurance policies, bank accounts, and investment accounts is essential to ensure that assets are distributed according to the individual's wishes and current family circumstances. Naming primary and contingent beneficiaries and updating designations after major life events helps avoid unintended consequences and ensures proper asset transfer.

4. Healthcare Directives: Executing healthcare directives, such as durable powers of attorney for healthcare and

living wills, allows individuals to designate healthcare proxies and provide instructions for medical treatment preferences in the event of incapacity. Healthcare directives ensure that individuals' wishes regarding end-of-life care and medical decision-making are respected and followed by healthcare providers and family members.

5. Tax Planning: Implementing tax planning strategies to minimize estate taxes, gift taxes, and income taxes is essential to preserve wealth and maximize asset transfer to future generations. Utilizing tax-efficient

estate planning techniques, such as gifting, charitable giving, estate freezing, and estate liquidity planning, helps individuals optimize tax outcomes and preserve assets for heirs and beneficiaries.

By proactively assessing retirement readiness, implementing strategies to build retirement savings, and executing comprehensive estate plans, individuals can secure their financial futures, protect their assets, and ensure the orderly transfer of wealth to future generations. With careful planning, informed decision-making, and professional guidance, individuals can navigate the complexities of retirement and estate planning with confidence, achieving peace of mind and financial security for themselves and their loved ones.

Chapter 9: Investment Planning

Now we will explore investment planning, a fundamental aspect of personal finance aimed at building wealth, achieving financial goals, and securing long-term financial security. Investment planning involves the strategic allocation of financial resources across various asset classes, such as stocks, bonds, real estate, and alternative investments, with the objective of maximizing returns while managing risk. This chapter provides readers with a comprehensive understanding of investment planning principles, portfolio construction strategies, risk management techniques, and the importance of disciplined investing for long-term wealth accumulation.

Understanding Investment Planning:

Investment planning is the process of identifying financial goals, assessing risk tolerance, and developing a customized investment strategy to achieve desired outcomes. Effective investment planning requires a thorough understanding of investment principles, market dynamics, economic trends, and individual preferences. By aligning investment strategies with financial objectives, time horizons, and risk profiles, investors can optimize portfolio performance and navigate market volatility with confidence.

Key Components of Investment Planning:

Investment planning encompasses several key components that form the foundation of a successful investment strategy:

1. Financial Goals: Identifying clear and specific financial goals is the first step in investment planning. Whether it's saving for retirement, funding education expenses, buying a home, or building a nest egg, defining financial objectives provides direction and purpose for investment decisions.

2. Risk Tolerance: Assessing risk tolerance involves understanding one's willingness and ability to tolerate fluctuations in investment returns and portfolio volatility. Risk tolerance is influenced by factors such as investment experience, time horizon, financial obligations, and

psychological factors. By aligning investment risk with risk tolerance, investors can create portfolios that balance growth potential with risk management.

3. Asset Allocation: Asset allocation is the strategic allocation of investment capital across different asset classes, such as stocks, bonds, cash, and alternative investments. Asset allocation decisions are based on investment goals, risk tolerance, time horizon, and market outlook. Diversification across asset classes helps spread risk and enhance risk-adjusted returns, reducing the impact

of market fluctuations on portfolio performance.

4. Portfolio Construction: Portfolio construction involves selecting specific investments within each asset class to build a well-diversified investment portfolio. Factors such as investment style, asset quality, sector exposure, geographic diversification, and cost considerations influence investment decisions. By combining complementary investments with low correlations, investors can reduce portfolio volatility and enhance overall returns.

5. Risk Management: Risk

management is an integral part of investment planning, focusing on identifying, assessing, and mitigating investment risks. Techniques such as asset allocation, diversification, hedging strategies, and periodic portfolio rebalancing help manage risk exposure and protect against potential losses. Risk management also involves monitoring market conditions, staying informed about economic trends, and adjusting investment strategies as needed to adapt to changing circumstances.

Investment Planning Strategies:

Investment planning strategies

encompass various approaches to portfolio construction, asset allocation, and risk management, tailored to meet individual objectives and preferences:

1. Long-Term Investing: Adopting a long-term investment horizon and maintaining a disciplined investment approach is essential for achieving investment success. Long-term investors benefit from the power of compounding, time diversification, and the ability to ride out short-term market fluctuations. By staying focused on long-term financial goals and avoiding reactionary decisions, investors can capitalize on market

opportunities and achieve superior investment results over time.

2. Diversification: Diversification is a cornerstone of investment planning, involving the allocation of assets across multiple asset classes, industries, and geographic regions. Diversified portfolios reduce concentration risk and minimize the impact of adverse events on investment performance. By spreading risk across different investments, investors can achieve a more stable and resilient portfolio that delivers consistent returns over the long term.

3. Asset Allocation: Asset allocation is

a key determinant of portfolio performance, with studies showing that asset allocation explains the majority of investment returns over time. Strategic asset allocation involves setting target allocations for different asset classes based on investment objectives, risk tolerance, and time horizon. By rebalancing portfolios periodically to maintain target allocations, investors can capture market opportunities and reduce portfolio drift.

4. Dollar-Cost Averaging: Dollar-cost averaging is an investment strategy that involves investing a fixed amount

of money at regular intervals, regardless of market conditions. This systematic approach to investing helps smooth out market volatility and reduce the impact of market fluctuations on investment returns. By consistently investing over time, investors can accumulate shares at varying price levels, resulting in a lower average cost per share and potentially higher returns over the long term.

5. Tax-Efficient Investing: Tax-efficient investing involves minimizing taxes on investment returns through strategies such as tax-loss harvesting, asset location optimization, and tax-deferred

accounts. By strategically positioning investments in tax-advantaged accounts, taking advantage of capital gains tax rates, and managing investment turnover, investors can maximize after-tax returns and enhance portfolio performance.

By understanding investment principles, setting clear financial goals, and implementing disciplined investment strategies, investors can navigate market uncertainties, manage investment risks, and achieve their financial objectives with confidence. With a focus on asset allocation, diversification, and risk management, investors can create portfolios that generate consistent returns, preserve capital, and secure financial futures for themselves and future generations.

Chapter 10:

Behavioral Finance and Market Behavior

Now we will delve into the fascinating field of behavioral finance and its implications for market behavior and investment decision-making. Behavioral finance explores how psychological biases, cognitive errors, and emotional factors influence investors' financial choices, market dynamics, and asset prices. This chapter provides readers with a comprehensive understanding of behavioral finance concepts, investor behavior patterns, and strategies for mitigating behavioral biases to make more rational and informed financial decisions.

Foundations of Behavioral Finance:

Behavioral finance challenges the traditional assumptions of classical finance, which posit that investors are rational, utility-maximizing individuals who make decisions based on all available information. Instead, behavioral finance acknowledges the presence of cognitive biases, emotional influences, and social factors that affect investors' perceptions, judgments, and decisions. By integrating insights from psychology, economics, and finance, behavioral finance seeks to understand how human behavior deviates from rationality and how these deviations impact market outcomes.

Key Concepts in Behavioral Finance:

Several key concepts and phenomena characterize behavioral finance and influence market behavior:

1. Cognitive Biases: Cognitive biases

are systematic errors in judgment and decision-making that arise from mental shortcuts, heuristics, and informational processing limitations. Common cognitive biases include confirmation bias, overconfidence, anchoring, loss aversion, and herding behavior, which lead investors to make suboptimal decisions and distort market prices.

2. Emotional Influences: Emotions play a significant role in financial decision-making, impacting investors' risk perception, investment preferences, and market participation. Emotional biases such as fear, greed, hope, and

regret influence investors' reactions to market events, leading to irrational behavior and market inefficiencies.

3. Prospect Theory: Prospect theory, developed by psychologists Daniel Kahneman and Amos Tversky, describes how individuals evaluate and make decisions under uncertainty. According to prospect theory, individuals are risk-averse when faced with gains but risk-seeking when faced with losses, leading to asymmetric risk preferences and deviations from rational decision-making.

4. Market Anomalies: Behavioral finance identifies various market

anomalies and inefficiencies that contradict the efficient market hypothesis (EMH). These anomalies, such as value premium, momentum effect, and investor sentiment, suggest that markets are not always efficient and may exhibit predictable patterns that can be exploited for investment gains.

Investor Behavior Patterns:

Understanding investor behavior patterns is essential for predicting market trends, assessing investor sentiment, and identifying potential investment opportunities. Common investor behavior patterns observed in financial markets include:

1. Herding Behavior: Herding behavior refers to the tendency of investors to follow the crowd and mimic the actions of others, rather than making independent decisions based on fundamental analysis or valuation metrics. Herding behavior can lead to market bubbles, speculative manias, and sudden price reversals as investors herd into or out of certain assets.

2. Overreaction and Underreaction: Behavioral finance theory suggests that investors tend to overreact to new information, causing asset prices to

overreact and deviate from their intrinsic value. Subsequently, markets may exhibit underreaction, where prices fail to fully adjust to new information, leading to mispricings and potential arbitrage opportunities for savvy investors.

3. Anchoring and Adjustment: Anchoring bias occurs when investors fixate on specific reference points or past events when making decisions, anchoring their judgments and estimates around these reference points. This bias can lead investors to underadjust their expectations in response to new information, resulting

in suboptimal decision-making and persistent market inefficiencies.

4. Disposition Effect: The disposition effect refers to investors' tendency to sell winning investments too early and hold onto losing investments too long. This behavior is driven by loss aversion and regret avoidance, as investors seek to realize gains and avoid admitting losses. The disposition effect can lead to suboptimal portfolio outcomes and hinder long-term wealth accumulation.

Strategies for Mitigating Behavioral Biases:

While behavioral biases are inherent in human decision-making, investors can adopt strategies to mitigate their impact and make more rational financial decisions:

1. Awareness and Education: Increasing awareness of common cognitive biases and emotional influences can help investors recognize and counteract irrational behavior. Education on behavioral finance concepts empowers investors to make more informed decisions and avoid falling prey to cognitive traps and emotional biases.

2. Objective Decision-Making:

Implementing objective decision-making processes, such as systematic investment strategies, rule-based approaches, and quantitative analysis, helps mitigate the influence of emotions and cognitive biases on investment decisions. By relying on predetermined criteria and data-driven methods, investors can make more disciplined and rational choices.

3. Long-Term Perspective: Maintaining a long-term investment horizon and focusing on fundamental factors and intrinsic value mitigate the impact of short-term market fluctuations and emotional reactions. A long-term

perspective allows investors to withstand market volatility, capitalize on investment opportunities, and achieve superior investment results over time.

4. Diversification and Risk Management: Diversifying investment portfolios across different asset classes, sectors, and geographic regions helps spread risk and reduce exposure to individual stocks or sectors affected by behavioral biases. Risk management techniques, such as stop-loss orders, position sizing, and asset allocation rebalancing, protect against excessive losses and preserve

capital during market downturns.

By recognizing cognitive biases, emotional influences, and investor behavior patterns, individuals can become more mindful investors and mitigate the negative effects of irrational decision-making. With awareness, education, and disciplined strategies, investors can navigate financial markets more effectively, capitalize on investment opportunities, and achieve their long-term financial goals with confidence and resilience.

Chapter 11:

The Practice of Investment

In this chapter, we will explore the practice of investment, focusing on the practical aspects of implementing investment strategies to achieve financial growth and wealth accumulation. Investment is a cornerstone of financial planning, allowing individuals to grow their assets, generate income, and achieve long-term financial goals. This chapter provides readers with practical insights into investment vehicles, portfolio management techniques, risk mitigation strategies, and the importance of disciplined execution in investment practice.

Understanding Investment Vehicles:

Investment vehicles are financial instruments or assets that individuals use to invest their money and generate returns. Common investment vehicles include:

1. Stocks: Stocks represent ownership stakes in publicly traded companies, offering investors the opportunity to

participate in company profits through dividends and capital appreciation. Stocks are suitable for investors seeking long-term growth potential and willing to accept market volatility.

2. Bonds: Bonds are debt securities issued by governments, corporations, or municipalities to raise capital. Bonds pay periodic interest payments to investors and return the principal amount at maturity. Bonds are valued for their income-generating potential, capital preservation, and diversification benefits in investment portfolios.

3. Mutual Funds: Mutual funds pool

money from multiple investors to invest in a diversified portfolio of stocks, bonds, or other securities. Mutual funds offer professional management, diversification, and liquidity, making them suitable for investors seeking a hands-off approach to investing.

4. Exchange-Traded Funds (ETFs): ETFs are investment funds traded on stock exchanges, tracking the performance of a specific index, sector, commodity, or asset class. ETFs offer low costs, intraday trading liquidity, and tax efficiency, making them popular among individual and

institutional investors for portfolio diversification and asset allocation.

5. Real Estate: Real estate investments involve owning, renting, or investing in residential, commercial, or industrial properties. Real estate offers potential for rental income, capital appreciation, and inflation protection, diversifying investment portfolios and providing alternative sources of returns.

Portfolio Management Techniques:

Effective portfolio management involves constructing and managing investment portfolios to achieve financial objectives while managing risk. Portfolio management techniques include:

1. Asset Allocation: Asset allocation is the strategic distribution of investment capital across different asset classes, such as stocks, bonds, and cash, based on investment goals, risk tolerance, and time horizon. Asset allocation determines portfolio risk and return characteristics and is a key driver of portfolio performance.

2. Diversification: Diversification involves spreading investment capital across multiple securities, asset classes, and geographic regions to reduce portfolio risk and enhance risk-

adjusted returns. Diversification minimizes the impact of individual security or sector-specific risks on portfolio performance and improves the consistency of investment outcomes.

3. Rebalancing: Rebalancing involves periodically adjusting portfolio asset allocations to maintain target investment weights and risk exposure. Rebalancing ensures that portfolios remain aligned with investment objectives, risk tolerance, and market conditions, preventing drift and optimizing portfolio performance over time.

4. Risk Management: Risk management techniques aim to identify, assess, and mitigate investment risks to protect capital and preserve wealth. Risk management strategies include diversification, asset allocation, hedging, stop-loss orders, and position sizing to minimize downside risk and manage volatility.

5. Tax Efficiency: Tax-efficient portfolio management involves minimizing taxes on investment returns through strategies such as asset location optimization, tax-loss harvesting, and tax-deferred account utilization. Tax-efficient investing

maximizes after-tax returns and enhances overall portfolio performance.

The Importance of Disciplined Execution:

Disciplined execution is crucial for successful investment practice, encompassing the following principles:

1. Goal Setting: Setting clear, specific, and measurable investment goals provides direction and motivation for investment decisions and helps track progress towards financial objectives.

2. Research and Analysis: Conducting thorough research and analysis of

investment opportunities, including fundamental analysis, technical analysis, and qualitative assessments, enables informed decision-making and identifies attractive investment opportunities.

3. Patience and Discipline: Exercising patience and discipline in investment practice involves adhering to investment strategies, resisting emotional impulses, and staying committed to long-term financial goals despite short-term market fluctuations.

4. Continuous Learning: Investing requires continuous learning and adaptation to evolving market

conditions, economic trends, and investment opportunities. Staying informed, seeking education, and learning from investment experiences are essential for improving investment outcomes over time.

5. Review and Adjustment: Regularly reviewing investment portfolios, performance metrics, and investment strategies allows investors to assess progress, identify areas for improvement, and make necessary adjustments to optimize investment outcomes and adapt to changing circumstances.

By understanding investment vehicles,

portfolio management techniques, and the importance of disciplined execution, individuals can build and manage investment portfolios to achieve their financial objectives with confidence and resilience. With a disciplined approach to investment practice, continuous learning, and a long-term perspective, investors can navigate financial markets effectively, capitalize on investment opportunities, and achieve long-term financial success and prosperity.

Chapter 12:
Owning Stocks

-Stocks and Stock Markets

Stocks and stock markets are the beating heart of the global economy, pulsating with the energy of millions of investors, traders, and companies striving to build wealth, innovate, and thrive in an ever-changing landscape. At their core, stocks represent ownership stakes in companies, granting shareholders a slice of the corporate pie and a voice in the boardroom. But beyond the tangible ownership rights, stocks embody the dreams, aspirations, and fortunes of individuals and institutions seeking financial growth and prosperity.

Stock markets serve as the bustling marketplaces where stocks are bought and sold, where supply meets demand, and where prices are determined by the collective wisdom (and occasional folly) of market participants. From the towering skyscrapers of Wall Street to the bustling trading floors of global exchanges, stock markets are the epicenters of capitalism, where capital flows freely and opportunities abound.

But what makes stocks and stock

markets so captivating? Perhaps it's the allure of potential wealth creation, where savvy investors can turn modest investments into fortunes through shrewd decision-making and astute timing. Or maybe it's the thrill of the chase, as traders seek to outsmart the market, ride the waves of momentum, and capture fleeting opportunities for profit.

Stock markets are also a reflection of human behavior, psychology, and sentiment. They embody the collective hopes, fears, and expectations of investors, as prices fluctuate in response to economic data, corporate earnings, geopolitical events, and investor sentiment. From the exuberance of bull markets to the despair of bear markets, stock markets mirror the ebb and flow of human emotions, driving prices to dizzying highs and gut-wrenching lows.

Investing in stocks is not without its risks, as volatility, uncertainty, and market gyrations are par for the course. Yet, for those willing to embrace the challenge, stocks offer the potential for long-term wealth creation, portfolio diversification, and inflation protection. With proper research, prudent risk management, and a long-term perspective, investors can harness the power of stocks to build a solid financial foundation and achieve their life goals.

Moreover, stocks play a vital role in fostering innovation, entrepreneurship, and economic growth. By providing companies with access to capital, stocks fuel investment in research and development, expansion initiatives, and job creation, driving innovation and progress across industries. From technology startups disrupting traditional business models to established blue-chip companies leading the charge in global markets, stocks empower companies to push the boundaries of what's possible and shape the future.

In the end, stocks and stock markets are more than just numbers on a screen or tickers flashing across a trading terminal. They are the lifeblood of capitalism, the engines of growth, and the embodiment of human ambition. Whether you're a seasoned investor navigating the complexities of the market or a novice dipping your toes into the world of stocks, one thing is certain: the journey of stocks and stock markets is an exhilarating ride filled with opportunities, challenges, and endless possibilities for those bold enough to seize them.

-Stock Value

Stock value, also known as stock price or equity value, is the market-determined price at which shares of a company's stock are bought and sold on a stock exchange. It represents the perceived worth of a company by investors and reflects a multitude of factors, including the company's financial performance, growth prospects, industry conditions, market sentiment, and macroeconomic trends.

At its essence, stock value is a

reflection of the present and anticipated future earnings potential of a company. Investors assess various financial metrics, such as earnings per share (EPS), price-to-earnings (P/E) ratio, price-to-book (P/B) ratio, and dividend yield, to gauge the intrinsic value of a stock relative to its market price. A stock's value is influenced by both quantitative factors, such as revenue growth, profit margins, and cash flow generation, as well as qualitative factors, such as management quality, competitive positioning, and industry trends.

The concept of stock value is deeply

rooted in the principles of valuation, which seek to determine the fair market price of a stock based on its underlying fundamentals. Valuation methodologies, such as discounted cash flow (DCF) analysis, relative valuation (comparable company analysis and precedent transactions), and asset-based valuation, provide investors with frameworks for estimating a company's intrinsic value and assessing its attractiveness as an investment opportunity.

However, stock value is not solely determined by objective financial metrics. It is also influenced by market dynamics, investor sentiment, and psychological factors. Market participants' perceptions, expectations, and emotions play a significant role in driving stock prices, leading to periods of overvaluation and undervaluation relative to a company's intrinsic worth.

Moreover, stock value is subject to volatility and fluctuation, as stock prices respond to changes in market conditions, economic data releases, geopolitical events, and company-specific news. Market participants' reactions to new information can cause stock prices to swing wildly in the short term, creating opportunities for investors to buy or sell stocks at attractive valuations.

In the long run, however, stock value tends to converge with a company's intrinsic value as market participants incorporate new information and adjust their expectations accordingly. Rational investors recognize that short-term fluctuations in stock prices may deviate from a company's true worth but ultimately believe that over time, stock prices will reflect underlying fundamentals.

Ultimately, understanding stock value requires a blend of financial analysis, market insights, and psychological awareness. Successful investors recognize that stock value is not static but dynamic, evolving in response to changing market conditions and investor perceptions. By conducting thorough research, exercising discipline, and maintaining a long-term perspective, investors can navigate the complexities of stock value and identify investment opportunities that align with their financial goals and risk tolerance.

-Common Measures of Value

In a world where value is often equated with monetary worth, it's crucial to expand our perspective and delve into the various dimensions that define value. Beyond mere price tags, there exists a rich tapestry of measures that encapsulate the worth of something, be it a product, service, or even an idea. Let's embark on a journey to explore these common measures of value:

1. Monetary Value: The most tangible and widely understood measure, monetary value represents the price of a commodity in currency. However, it's important to recognize that monetary value doesn't always reflect the true worth of something. Factors such as scarcity, demand, and utility play

significant roles in determining monetary value.

2. Utility Value: Utility value assesses the usefulness or functionality of a product or service to its consumer. It's about how much satisfaction or benefit an individual derives from using or owning something. For example, a tool that improves efficiency or a service that saves time holds high utility value.

3. Emotional Value: Emotions often influence our perception of value. Products or experiences that evoke positive emotions such as joy, nostalgia, or belonging tend to be

valued more highly by consumers. Brands often leverage emotional value through storytelling, branding, and creating experiences that forge connections with their audience.

4. Social Value: Social value refers to the significance something holds within a community or society. This can encompass cultural relevance, social status, or contribution to social well-being. For instance, a piece of art may hold social value by reflecting cultural identity or sparking important conversations.

5. Environmental Value: With increasing awareness of

environmental issues, the environmental value of products and services is gaining prominence. This measure considers the impact of a product or service on the environment, including factors like sustainability, carbon footprint, and ecological preservation.

6. Quality Value: Quality value relates to the level of excellence or superiority inherent in a product or service. It encompasses factors such as durability, craftsmanship, reliability, and performance. Consumers often associate higher quality with greater value, even if it comes with a higher

price tag.

7. Time Value: Time is a precious resource, and its value extends beyond mere monetary terms. Time value considers factors such as convenience, speed of delivery, and time saved. In today's fast-paced world, products and services that save time or streamline processes hold significant value for consumers.

8. Cognitive Value: Cognitive value pertains to the intellectual or educational benefits derived from a product or service. This could include learning opportunities, mental stimulation, or access to information

that enriches one's understanding or skills.

By recognizing and understanding these diverse measures of value, individuals and businesses can make more informed decisions, create products and services that resonate with their audience, and contribute to a more nuanced understanding of worth in society. Ultimately, value is multifaceted, dynamic, and deeply subjective, reflecting the complexity of human needs, desires, and aspirations.

-Equity Strategies

Equity strategies serve as the

cornerstone of investment portfolios, offering a pathway to potential growth, income, and wealth accumulation. In the dynamic landscape of financial markets, mastering these strategies requires a blend of foresight, analysis, and adaptability. Let's embark on a journey to explore the realm of equity strategies and unveil the tactics that empower investors to navigate with precision:

1. Value Investing: Championed by legendary investors like Warren Buffett and Benjamin Graham, value investing involves identifying undervalued

stocks trading below their intrinsic worth. Investors scour the markets for companies with strong fundamentals, stable earnings, and healthy balance sheets, often overlooked by the broader market sentiment. By purchasing these stocks at a discount, value investors aim to capitalize on their eventual rise to fair value, realizing significant gains in the process.

2. Growth Investing: Contrary to value investing, growth investing focuses on companies poised for rapid expansion and capital appreciation. Investors gravitate towards firms demonstrating

robust revenue growth, disruptive innovation, and scalability potential. While growth stocks may command premium valuations, investors are willing to pay a premium in anticipation of future earnings growth and market dominance.

3. Dividend Investing: For investors seeking a steady stream of income, dividend investing offers an attractive avenue. This strategy involves selecting stocks from companies that consistently distribute a portion of their profits to shareholders in the form of dividends. Dividend-paying stocks often belong to mature, stable

companies with strong cash flows and a history of dividend growth. By reinvesting dividends or using them as a source of passive income, investors can enhance portfolio returns and mitigate market volatility.

4. Sector Rotation: Sector rotation entails rotating investments across different sectors of the economy based on macroeconomic trends, business cycles, and sector-specific catalysts. Investors capitalize on sector rotation by identifying industries poised for outperformance while reducing exposure to sectors facing headwinds or cyclical

downturns. This strategy requires a keen understanding of market dynamics, economic indicators, and sector-specific drivers to effectively allocate capital and capture upside potential.

5. Momentum Investing: Momentum investing capitalizes on the phenomenon of price trends persisting over time. Investors identify stocks exhibiting strong price momentum and enter positions with the expectation that the trend will continue in the short to medium term. Momentum strategies leverage technical analysis, market breadth indicators, and relative

strength metrics to identify high-probability trade opportunities and capitalize on market inefficiencies.

6. Contrarian Investing: Contrarian investing involves swimming against the tide of prevailing market sentiment, buying when others are selling and selling when others are buying. Contrarian investors seek out-of-favor stocks trading at depressed valuations due to temporary setbacks, market overreactions, or negative sentiment. By maintaining a contrarian stance, investors can capitalize on market mispricing and position themselves for substantial gains as sentiment

reverses.

7. Quantitative Investing: Quantitative investing harnesses the power of data analytics, mathematical models, and algorithmic trading to identify and exploit market inefficiencies. Quantitative strategies leverage quantitative factors such as price movements, earnings surprises, and statistical anomalies to generate alpha and optimize portfolio returns. This data-driven approach combines rigorous research with advanced statistical techniques to uncover hidden patterns and gain a competitive edge in the markets.

By mastering these equity strategies and adapting them to suit individual risk tolerance, investment objectives, and market conditions, investors can navigate the complexities of the financial markets with confidence and precision. Whether seeking capital appreciation, income generation, or risk diversification, the art of equity strategies offers a versatile toolkit for achieving financial success in an ever-evolving investment landscape.

Chapter 13:

Investing in Mutual Funds, Commodities, Real Estate, and Collectibles

-Mutual Funds

Mutual funds have long been hailed as one of the most accessible and effective tools for wealth creation. But what exactly are mutual funds, and why are they such a popular choice among investors? Let's embark on a journey to uncover the secrets behind the success of mutual funds and how they can pave the way for your financial prosperity.

Understanding Mutual Funds:

At its core, a mutual fund is a pool of money collected from numerous investors to invest in various securities such as stocks, bonds, money market instruments, and other assets. This pooled capital is managed by professional fund managers who make investment decisions on behalf of the investors. By spreading investments across a diversified portfolio, mutual funds aim to mitigate risk while maximizing returns.

Diverse Range of Options:

One of the key attractions of mutual funds is the sheer diversity of options available. Whether you're a conservative investor seeking stability or an aggressive investor chasing high returns, there's a mutual fund suited to your risk appetite and financial goals. From equity funds that invest in stocks to fixed-income funds that focus on bonds, and even hybrid funds that blend both asset classes, the choices are virtually limitless.

Professional Management:

Unlike individual investors who may lack the time, expertise, or resources to manage their investments effectively, mutual funds offer access to seasoned professionals with a deep understanding of the financial markets. These fund managers conduct in-depth research, analyze market trends, and execute investment strategies with the aim of generating optimal returns for investors. Their expertise can help navigate volatile market conditions and seize lucrative opportunities.

Diversification Benefits:

The age-old adage "don't put all your eggs in one basket" rings true in the world of investing, and mutual funds excel in this regard. By spreading investments across a wide range of securities, mutual funds reduce the impact of any single asset's poor performance on the overall portfolio. This diversification not only lowers risk but also enhances the potential for long-term growth.

Accessibility and Affordability:

Gone are the days when investing in the financial markets was reserved for the privileged few. Mutual funds offer a low barrier to entry, allowing even novice investors to participate with modest sums of money. With options like systematic investment plans (SIPs), investors can start investing regularly with as little as a few hundred rupees, making wealth creation more accessible than ever before.

Transparency and Liquidity:

Investing in mutual funds provides transparency regarding the fund's holdings, performance, and expenses. Investors receive regular updates on their investments, enabling them to make informed decisions. Moreover, mutual funds offer liquidity, allowing investors to buy or sell units at the prevailing Net Asset Value (NAV) on any business day, providing flexibility and convenience.

Mutual funds stand as a beacon of hope for individuals aspiring to build wealth and achieve their financial goals. With their diverse range of options, professional management, diversification benefits, accessibility, transparency, and liquidity, mutual funds offer a compelling proposition for investors seeking to harness the power of the financial markets. Whether you're planning for retirement, saving for a child's education, or simply aiming to grow your wealth, mutual funds can serve as your trusted ally on the path to financial success.

-Real Estate Investments

Real estate investment is more than just buying property; it's a gateway to financial freedom and long-term wealth accumulation. From residential homes to commercial buildings, the real estate market offers diverse opportunities for investors to grow their portfolios and secure their financial futures.

1. Diversification and Stability:

Real estate investments provide a hedge against market volatility. Unlike stocks and bonds, which can fluctuate wildly, real estate tends to be more stable over time. Diversifying your investment portfolio with real estate assets can help reduce overall risk and enhance stability, especially during economic downturns.

2. Passive Income Streams:

One of the most attractive features of real estate investments is the potential for generating passive income. Rental properties, in particular, offer investors a steady stream of cash flow through monthly rental payments. With careful property selection and management, investors can build a portfolio of income-producing assets that provide financial security and independence.

3. Appreciation and Equity Build-Up:

Over time, real estate properties have historically appreciated in value, providing investors with significant returns on their initial investment. Additionally, as mortgage payments are made and property values increase, investors build equity in their properties, further enhancing their net worth. This combination of appreciation and equity build-up can result in substantial long-term wealth accumulation.

4. Tax Advantages:

Real estate investments offer numerous tax benefits that can help investors maximize their returns and minimize their tax liabilities. Tax deductions for mortgage interest, property taxes, depreciation, and maintenance expenses can significantly reduce the amount of taxable income generated by real estate investments. Additionally, investors may benefit from capital gains tax deferral through like-kind exchanges and tax-free appreciation upon property sale through 1031 exchanges.

5. Inflation Hedge:

Real estate investments have historically served as an effective hedge against inflation. As the cost of goods and services rises over time, so do property values and rental incomes. This means that real estate investments have the potential to maintain or even increase in value in tandem with inflation, preserving investors' purchasing power and wealth.

Real estate investments offer a multitude of benefits, from diversification and passive income to appreciation and tax advantages.

Whether you're a seasoned investor or just starting out, incorporating real estate into your investment strategy can help you unlock wealth and achieve your financial goals. With careful planning, due diligence, and a long-term perspective, real estate investments can pave the way to financial independence and prosperity.

-Commodities and Collectibles

In the realm of investment, stocks and bonds often take center stage. However, there exists a fascinating and diverse universe of alternative investments that offer unique opportunities for growth and diversification. Among these are commodities and collectibles, two asset classes that have captured the attention of investors seeking to broaden their portfolios and enhance their returns.

1. Commodities: The Cornerstone of Global Markets

Commodities represent essential raw materials or primary agricultural products that are traded on global exchanges. From precious metals like gold and silver to energy sources such as oil and natural gas, commodities play a pivotal role in the global economy. Investing in commodities provides investors with exposure to fundamental market forces, including supply and demand dynamics, geopolitical events, and macroeconomic trends.

2. Diversification and Inflation Protection

Commodities offer an excellent diversification tool for investors looking to hedge against traditional market risks. Unlike stocks and bonds, which are influenced by factors such as interest rates and company performance, commodity prices are driven by a distinct set of supply and demand fundamentals. Additionally, commodities have historically served as a hedge against inflation, as their prices tend to rise during periods of currency devaluation and rising prices.

3. Collectibles: Investing in Passion and Profit

Collectibles encompass a wide range of tangible assets, including art, antiques, rare coins, stamps, and vintage cars. While these items may hold sentimental value for collectors, they also represent valuable investment opportunities. Collectibles often appreciate in value over time, driven by factors such as scarcity, historical significance, and cultural relevance. Investing in collectibles allows investors to combine their passion for art, history, or craftsmanship with the potential for financial gain.

4. Tangible Assets and Portfolio Diversification

Collectibles offer investors a unique form of diversification by providing exposure to tangible assets that are not directly correlated with traditional financial markets. In times of market volatility or economic uncertainty, collectibles can serve as a store of value and a source of stability within an investment portfolio. Additionally, collectibles offer the potential for significant returns, as demonstrated by record-breaking auction prices for fine art and rare collectible items.

5. Due Diligence and Market Expertise

Investing in commodities and collectibles requires a thorough understanding of market dynamics, valuation methodologies, and industry trends. Successful investors in these asset classes often possess specialized knowledge or work closely with trusted advisors who can provide insights into market opportunities and risks. Conducting thorough due diligence and staying informed about market developments are essential steps in building a successful portfolio of commodities and collectibles.

Commodities and collectibles offer investors unique opportunities to diversify their portfolios, hedge against traditional market risks, and potentially achieve attractive returns. Whether you're interested in the dynamic world of commodity trading or the timeless appeal of rare collectible items, exploring alternative investments can open doors to new avenues of wealth creation and financial security. With careful research, prudent decision-making, and a long-term perspective, investors can unlock the potential of commodities and collectibles to enhance their investment strategies and achieve their financial goals.

Chapter 14:

Career Planning

-Choosing a Job

Selecting the right job isn't just about earning a paycheck; it's about finding a role that aligns with your skills, values, and long-term career aspirations. With countless opportunities available in today's job market, navigating the process of choosing a job can be both exciting and overwhelming. However, by considering key factors and conducting thorough self-assessment, you can uncover the perfect professional fit.

1. Self-Assessment: Know Thyself

Before embarking on your job search journey, take the time to conduct a thorough self-assessment. Reflect on your strengths, skills, interests, and values. Consider what motivates you, what type of work environment you thrive in, and what you envision for your future career trajectory. Understanding your unique preferences and priorities will help you narrow down your job options and identify opportunities that are well-suited to your individual profile.

2. Define Your Career Goals

Set clear and achievable career goals that align with your interests and aspirations. Whether you're seeking opportunities for professional growth, leadership development, or work-life balance, having a clear vision of what you want to achieve will guide your job search efforts. Consider both short-term and long-term objectives, and look for roles that offer opportunities for advancement and skill development in line with your career goals.

3. Research and Explore Options

Take the time to research and explore different job opportunities and industries. Look beyond job titles and delve into the day-to-day responsibilities, company culture, and growth prospects of potential employers. Leverage online resources, professional networks, informational interviews, and job shadowing experiences to gain insights into various roles and organizations. Be open to exploring different career paths and industries that align with your interests and goals.

4. Evaluate Company Culture and Values

Company culture plays a significant role in job satisfaction and overall happiness in the workplace. Evaluate potential employers based on their values, mission, and workplace culture. Consider factors such as work-life balance, employee benefits, diversity and inclusion initiatives, and opportunities for professional development and mentorship. Look for organizations that foster a supportive and inclusive work environment where you can thrive and grow professionally.

5. Consider Compensation and Benefits

While salary and benefits are

important considerations when choosing a job, they should not be the sole determining factors. Evaluate compensation packages holistically, taking into account factors such as health insurance, retirement plans, bonuses, and perks. Consider the overall value proposition of the job, including opportunities for advancement, learning and development resources, and work-life balance initiatives.

Choosing a job is a significant decision that can impact your career trajectory and overall well-being. By conducting thorough self-assessment, defining your career goals, researching potential employers, evaluating company culture, and considering compensation and benefits, you can make informed decisions that align with your values and aspirations. Remember that finding the perfect professional fit may require time and exploration, but with patience and perseverance, you can discover a rewarding career path that brings fulfillment and success.

-Finding a Job

Embarking on the quest to find a job is an exhilarating journey filled with opportunities for growth, discovery, and professional fulfillment. Whether you're a recent graduate launching your career or an experienced professional seeking new challenges, the process of finding a job is an adventure that requires preparation, perseverance, and a sense of curiosity. Let's dive into the exciting world of job hunting and uncover the keys to success.

1. Define Your Path: Know What You Want

Before setting out on your job search journey, take the time to define your career goals and aspirations. Reflect on your skills, interests, and values to identify the type of role and industry that aligns with your strengths and passions. Consider factors such as job function, company culture, location, and growth opportunities. Having a clear sense of direction will guide your job search efforts and increase your chances of finding a job that's the right fit for you.

2. Polish Your Tools: Craft a Standout Resume and Cover Letter

Your resume and cover letter are your first impression with potential employers, so it's essential to make them stand out. Tailor your resume to highlight your relevant skills, experiences, and achievements that demonstrate your qualifications for the job. Use concise language, bullet points, and quantifiable results to showcase your accomplishments. Similarly, craft a compelling cover letter that expresses your enthusiasm for the role and company while articulating how your background and skills align with the job requirements.

3. Network Like a Pro: Tap Into Your Connections

Networking is a powerful tool for uncovering job opportunities and gaining insights into different industries and companies. Leverage your existing network of friends, family, classmates, colleagues, and mentors to seek advice, referrals, and informational interviews. Attend networking events, industry conferences, and professional meetups to expand your circle of contacts and learn from others in your field. Building meaningful relationships can open doors to hidden job opportunities and provide valuable guidance throughout your job search journey.

4. Embrace the Digital Landscape: Harness the Power of Online Platforms

In today's digital age, online platforms play a crucial role in the job search process. Create a strong presence on professional networking sites like LinkedIn, where you can showcase your skills, experiences, and professional accomplishments. Join industry-specific groups and participate in discussions to establish yourself as a thought leader in your field. Additionally, leverage job search websites, company career portals, and online job boards to discover job openings and submit your applications.

5. Stay Resilient and Persistent: Embrace the Journey

Finding a job can be a challenging and sometimes lengthy process, but it's essential to stay resilient and persistent. Rejection is a natural part of the job search process, so don't be discouraged by setbacks. Stay focused on your goals, maintain a positive attitude, and continue to adapt and refine your job search strategy based on feedback and insights gained along the way. Remember that each step of the journey brings valuable learning experiences and opportunities for personal and professional growth.

Finding a job is an adventure filled with

excitement, challenges, and opportunities. By defining your path, polishing your tools, networking like a pro, embracing the digital landscape, and staying resilient and persistent, you can navigate the job search journey with confidence and purpose. Keep an open mind, be proactive in your approach, and trust in your abilities to uncover the perfect opportunity that aligns with your goals and aspirations. The adventure begins now—happy job hunting!

www.ingramcontent.com/pod-product-compliance
Lightning Source LLC
Chambersburg PA
CBHW052149220526
45471CB00004B/1589